Prince Charming?

...or TOAD-ally Alarming?

Jennifer Fox

Illustrated by Frank Montagna

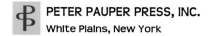

PETER PAUPER PRESS, INC.

White Plains, New York

For Prince Marcus,
my favorite amphibian

Designed by Heather Zschock

Illustrations copyright © 2007 Frank Montagna/www.artscounselinc.com

Copyright © 2007
Peter Pauper Press, Inc.
202 Mamaroneck Avenue
White Plains, NY 10601
All rights reserved
ISBN 978-1-59359-879-2
Printed in China
7 6 5 4 3 2 1

Visit us at www.peterpauper.com

Prince Charming?

...or TOAD-ally Alarming?

Introduction

Every woman knows the old adage: *You have to kiss a lot of toads before you find a prince.* And while we'd like to believe it's just an old wives' tale—all too often it turns out to be true. That guy who seemed so great on a first date begins to show his truly toad-ish ways after just a few weeks. In no time, your would-be prince is a full-fledged frog. What's a savvy single gal to do when the dating scene is awash in amphibians, and your pucker and patience are growing wart-weary?

Take heart—your new fairy godmother has arrived! *Prince Charming?…or TOAD-ally Alarming?* is every single's salvation. This purse-sized primer is packed with page after page of entertaining yet informative pairings, comparing behavior that's worthy of prince charming and that which is toad-ally alarming. The guesswork is all done for you. Simply heed these warning signs to dodge that toad and discover the princely partner every modern girl truly deserves.

So dive back into the dating pond with confidence. Banish that tired old adage back to once-upon-a-time where it belongs, and sink toad-kissing to the murky depths for good. With all the precious hours you'll save "trying on" men, you'll have plenty of time left over for positively princessly pursuits (like trying on shoes)! Just be sure to watch out for those pesky glass slippers!

PRINCE:

Pays for coffee.

TOAD:

Pays for coffee out of the tip jar.

PRINCE:

Buys you your
favorite
movie candy.

T O A D :

Makes you

smuggle it in

your purse.

PRINCE:

It's obvious he loves his mother.

TOAD:

It's obvious he lives
with his mother.

P R I N C E :

Calls you the
next day.

TOAD:

Calls you the wrong name.

PRINCE:

Mentions his best friend—

He must get along well with others.

TOAD:

Mentions his best friend

is a ferret named Mr. Wiggles.

PRINCE:

Invites you over to his place to show off his culinary skills.

TOAD:

Invites you over to his place to avoid setting off his ankle bracelet.

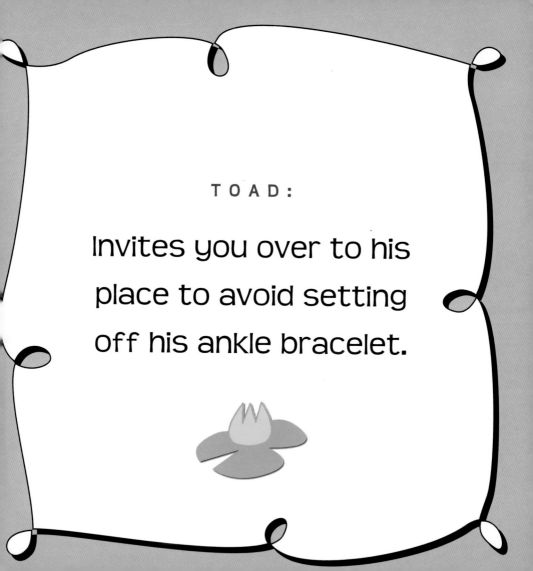

PRINCE:

He looks like he
just stepped off
a movie set...

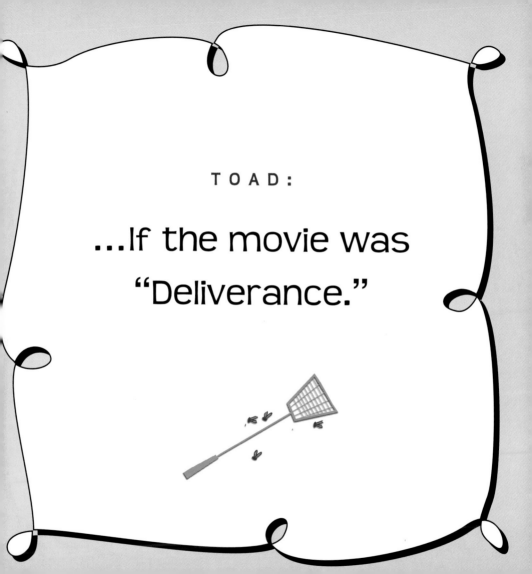

PRINCE:

Leaves the waitress
a good tip.

TOAD:

Leaves the waitress
his cell number.

PRINCE:

Brings flowers on

the first date.

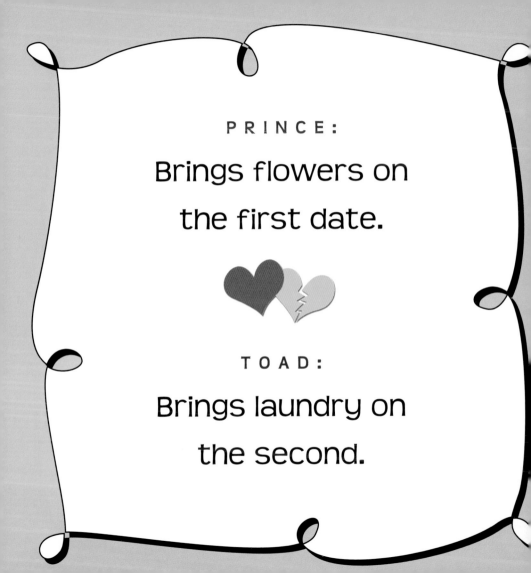

TOAD:

Brings laundry on

the second.

APT
14G

PRINCE:

Steals your heart.

T O A D :

Steals your stereo.

PRINCE:

Offers to rub
your back.

TOAD:

Asks you to

wax his.

PRINCE:

Travels for
business.

T O A D :

Travels for "Star Trek"
conventions.

PRINCE:

He's writing the great American novel.

TOAD:

It's a true-crime
autobiography.

PRINCE:

He thinks your age
difference is great—
He likes a woman
who's older and wiser.

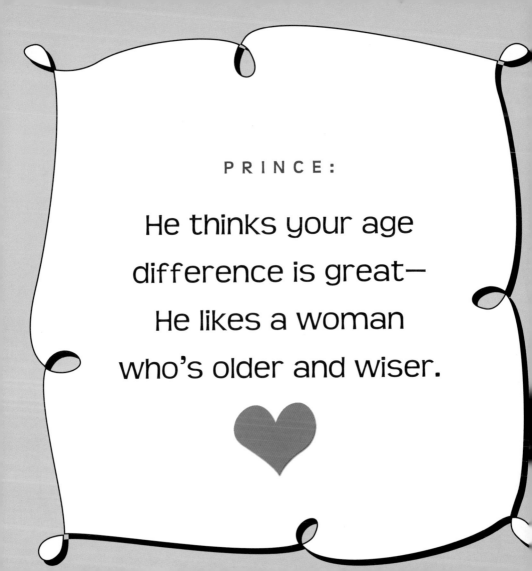

TOAD:

He thinks your age
difference is great—
He likes a woman who
can buy him beer.

PRINCE:

Takes you out

for sushi.

TOAD:

Refers to your
dinner as "bait."

PRINCE:

Waits to call you back
when the football
game is over.

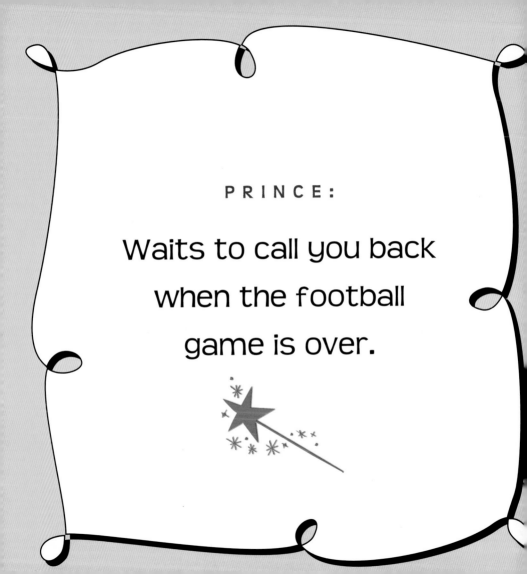

T O A D :

Waits to call you back
when the football
SEASON is over.

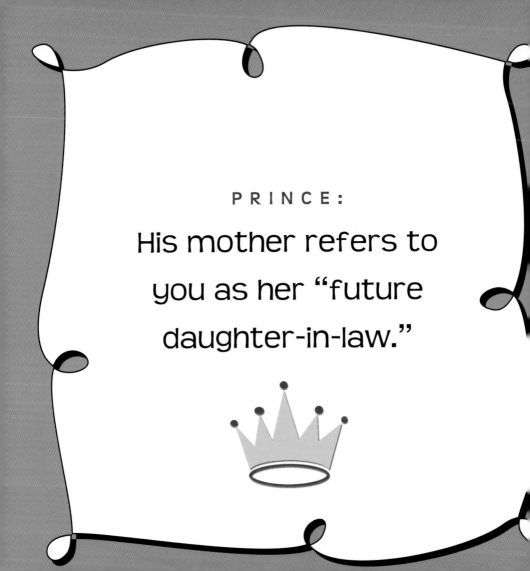

PRINCE:

His mother refers to you as her "future daughter-in-law."

TOAD:

His mother refers
to you as the
"other woman."

PRINCE:

He's not afraid to cry when you watch a sad movie.

TOAD:

He's not afraid to cry when you beat him at golf.

Mentions he has family

in the Midwest.

T O A D :

Doesn't mention it's

a wife and kids.

PRINCE:

Head hunters are
after him.

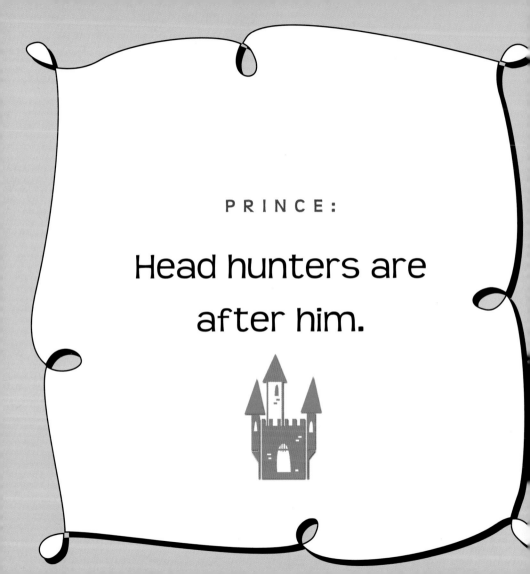

TOAD:

Bounty hunters are after him.

T O A D :

Does his own
taxidermy.

PRINCE:

Brings you

breakfast in bed.

TOAD:

Eats potato chips in bed.

You share the same
taste in movies.

You share the same
taste in underwear.

PRINCE:

Saw his picture
in the "Wall Street
Journal."

T O A D :

Saw his picture in
the post office.

T O A D :

Passed OUT
at the bar.

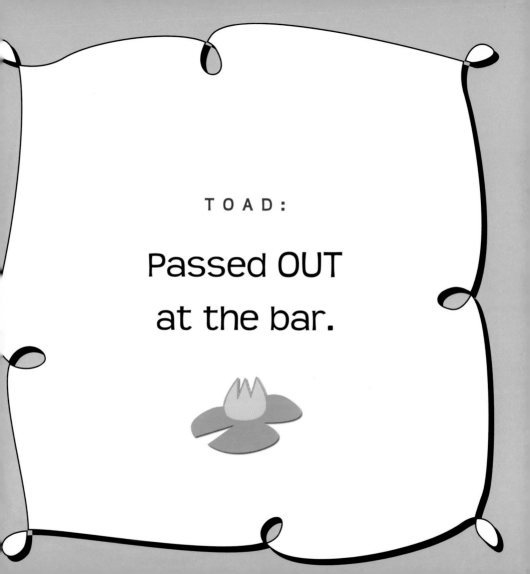

PRINCE:

Offers to take out
your trash.

PRINCE:

Invites you to poker night—
He knows you can hang
with the guys.

TOAD:

Invites you to poker night—
Someone's got to serve
the snacks.

PRINCE:

Takes you home
to meet his mom
and sister.

TOAD:

She's the same
person.

PRINCE:

There are no
awkward silences
on your date.

T O A D :

He's too busy talking
about himself.

PRINCE:

Has a history of
being in committed
relationships.

TOAD:

Has a history of
being committed.

PRINCE:

Laughs at your jokes.

TOAD:

Laughs at your outfit.

PRINCE:

Looks like a
male model.

T O A D :

Acts like a
male model.

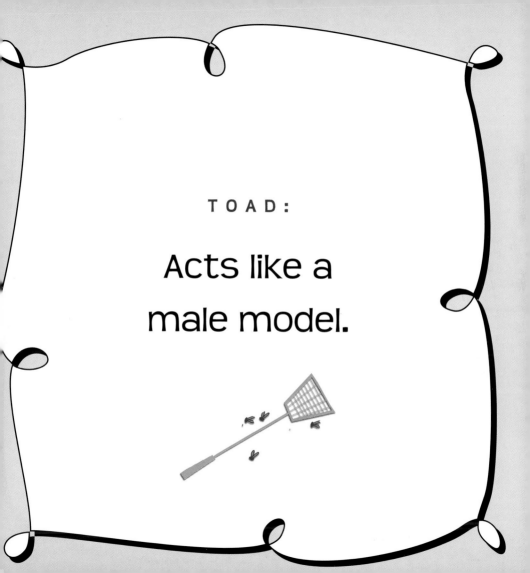

PRINCE:

Takes you to his friend's party and refers to you as his "girlfriend."

T O A D :

Takes you to a medieval theme

restaurant and refers

to you as his "wench."

PRINCE:

He speaks
two languages.

T O A D :

One of them is
Neanderthal.

PRINCE:

Describes himself

as athletic.

TOAD:

Counts video games

as a sport.

PRINCE:

Looks like
Ben Affleck online.

T O A D :

Looks like
Ben Franklin in person.

PRINCE:

Lets you pick out
the restaurant.

TOAD:

Lets you pick
up the tab.

PRINCE:

He thinks French restaurants are romantic.

T O A D :

He thinks French
maids are romantic.

PRINCE:

"Six pack"

refers to his abs.

TOAD:

"Six pack" refers
to his breakfast.

PRINCE:

He has a career in journalism.

TOAD:

It's a paper route.